T0065105

CHOOSING YOUR BATTLES

CHOOSING YOUR BATTLES

INSPIRATION AND WISDOM
FROM A NAVY SEAL ON
HOW TO WIN YOUR BATTLES AND
ENSURE A POSITIVE OUTCOME

DON MANN
WITH KRAIG BECKER

Skyhorse Publishing

Skyhorse Publishing books may be purchased in bulk at special discounts for sales promotion, corporate gifts, fund-raising, or educational purposes. Special editions can also be created to specifications. For details, contact the Special Sales Department, Skyhorse Publishing, 307 West 36th Street, 11th Floor, New York, NY 10018 or info@skyhorsepublishing.com.

Skyhorse® and Skyhorse Publishing® are registered trademarks of Skyhorse Publishing, Inc.®, a Delaware corporation.

Visit our website at www.skyhorsepublishing.com.

10 9 8 7 6 5 4 3 2 1

Library of Congress Cataloging-in-Publication Data is available on file.

Cover design by Brian Peterson

Print ISBN: 978-1-5107-5204-7
Ebook ISBN: 978-1-5107-4578-0

Printed in China

CONTENTS

PART I

DRAWING A LINE IN THE SAND

On August 2, 1990, Iraqi forces, under orders from Saddam Hussein, invaded the neighboring country of Kuwait. The dictator's goal was to seize Kuwaiti oil fields and quickly take control of the country's petroleum production facilities. By disrupting output from those refineries Hussein could force the price of oil to increase sharply on the international markets, lining his pockets with the profits as a result.

Woefully outnumbered, outgunned, and outmatched, the Kuwaiti forces were soundly defeated in just two days. Iraq's Republican Guard ruthlessly smashed all resistance, wiping the opposition from the battlefield. Some Kuwaiti units fled into nearby Saudi Arabia and Bahrain to escape destruction or capture, but most were eliminated within hours of the start of the invasion.

Iraq's aggressive attack on its neighbor was quickly and resoundingly condemned by the international community. Within days, the United Nations approved economic sanctions against the

Middle Eastern country, and a naval blockade was soon put in place to keep vital supplies from reaching Iraqi shores. But Hussein remained unfazed and settled in for what looked like a protracted conflict. He argued that Kuwait was historically a part of Iraq anyway and that he was only reclaiming what was rightfully his.

A weeks-long standoff ensued, during which Iraqi forces dug in and hardened their positions in Kuwait. Meanwhile, an international coalition—led by the United States—began to build up its presence in the region. As the months passed, more than 900,000 troops were sent to Saudi Arabia and other nearby countries in anticipation of an armed clash. For the US, it was the largest deployment of its armed forces since the Vietnam War, with the Navy sending two full battle groups into the Persian Gulf. Meanwhile, the US Air Force dispatched fighter planes and bombers to help patrol the skies, and the Army prepared for a deadly showdown with Iraq's well-trained and well-equipped forces.

Tensions ran high on both sides, with negotiations, eventually breaking down altogether. Hussein refused to withdraw his troops from Kuwait, while the growing allied coalition would accept no other course of action. On November 29, the United Nations passed a resolution authorizing the use of military force if Iraq did not exit Kuwait by January 15, 1991. In a sense, the resolution put Saddam and his forces on the clock, giving them a hard deadline for when to relinquish control over the captured territory.

Eventually that deadline came and went and, as promised, the US and its allies launched Operation Desert Storm. The plan was to conduct a systematic and controlled air campaign against the Iraqi army, eliminating its ability to maintain a high level of defense. For five weeks allied aircraft bombarded strategic locations across Kuwait, destroying Iraqi equipment, personnel, and moral. The bombing raids were conducted day and night, often with precision accuracy and devastating results.

The air campaign served as the precursor to Operation Desert Saber, which, on February 24, saw allied ground forces invade Kuwait with the goal of expelling the Iraqis. After weeks of intense attacks from the sky, Saddam's military—including the elite Republican Guard—were severely weakened and soon beat a hasty retreat. In their wake they left death and destruction, setting fire to hundreds of Kuwaiti oil fields and destroying crucial infrastructure as they went.

The ground portion of the Gulf War was over in a manner of just a few days. Within 100 hours of the start of Operation Desert Saber, the Iraqi army had either been destroyed or had retreated across the border. Thousands of enemy soldiers were captured or killed, with Iraqi tanks, armored cars, aircraft, and other vehicles littering the battlefield.

Saddam Hussein suffered a resounding defeat with his troops being expelled just as quickly as they had captured Kuwait only seven months earlier. It was an impressive display of US military might, although the allied forces played an important part in helping to liberate the captured nation.

As you can probably imagine, US Navy SEALs had a crucial role during the Gulf War. In fact, long before the allies began building up their forces, SEALs were already on the scene and conducting important operations. Within days of the Iraqi invasion, President George H. W. Bush ordered the start of Operation Desert Shield, which set in motion plans to escalate a military build-up in the region. It would take months for those plans to fully come together, but in the meantime the SEALs were already scouting the area, conducting sabotage missions and boarding incoming ships to inspect for contraband.

Early on the SEALs also served as instructors and advisors. As some of the first US personnel on the ground in Saudi Arabia, SEAL team members showed the Saudi military how to effectively call in air strikes and bombing raids in preparation for their defense. Those lessons would prove invaluable once the Gulf War officially got underway, assisting pilots in locating and eliminating important enemy targets.

Once Operation Desert Storm began on January 17, the SEALs turned their focus to other matters. One of their most important jobs was to identify and map the location of Iraqi mines that had been deployed along the Kuwaiti coast to help fend off an amphibious assault. They would also conduct nightly recon missions to not only assess enemy strength and readiness but to observe the impact that the air war was having on Saddam's forces.

Those missions typically began 500 meters from shore, where the SEALs would silently slip into the water and swim toward the beach. Water temperatures typically hovered around 50°F and the surface of the Persian Gulf had a layer of oil on it at all times, making the missions far from comfortable or easy. Still, the SEALs provided critical intelligence that would later assist allied forces when they launched the ground assault in February.

"

The battles that count aren't the ones for gold medals. The struggles within yourself, the invisible, inevitable battles inside all of us, that's where it's at."

—Jesse Owens

Perhaps the most important role that Navy SEALs played in the Gulf War was to set up a highly effective diversion to distract key Iraqi units. As Operation Desert Storm was starting to wind down, and the launch of Operation Desert Saber was imminent, a plan was drafted that could potentially shorten the conflict and save thousands of lives. That plan involved setting off explosives along the Kuwaiti coast in an attempt to convince the enemy that an amphibious assault was underway. If done correctly, it could divert the attention of Saddam's forces, drawing them away from the real invasion, which was set to arrive by land instead.

On the night of February 24, just as the allies were planning to invade Kuwait, members of SEAL Team Five embarked on an important mission too. They traveled seventy miles by boat to reach a strategic beach where they stealthily swam to shore and planted a series of demolitions. After this mission was completed, they exited the area of operation (AO) without the enemy even knowing they were ever there.

Once they were safely aboard their high-speed boats, the team approached the shore and made a very loud and impressive display of force. They fired their weapons at Iraqi bunkers and threw satchel charges into the water to create the illusion that something big was happening. Then, just before they sped away, they detonated the charges that had previously been set on shore. To the startled enemy soldiers it appeared as if the US Navy and its allies were about to make a full-scale invasion of the beach.

The diversion was a major success. According to US intelligence, two Iraqi armored divisions left their fortified positions in order to fend off the nonexistent assault that never came. With those forces out of the way, the actual invading army met with significantly less resistance, allowing their initial attack to come as a significant surprise. Caught unaware, the Iraqi forces suffered heavy casualties as the allied forces moved forward.

As ground operations got underway, the SEALs continued to play a crucial part in the conflict. Because of their intense training and incredible versatility in battlefield operations, they were called upon to handle unique situations while the main invasion force was occupied elsewhere. For instance, a group of SEALs rescued an American pilot who was shot down behind enemy lines and helped retake a small island located in the Persian Gulf, capturing more than fifty Iraqi POWs in the process.

Shortly after the invasion of Kuwait began back in August, President Bush addressed a joint session of Congress to inform them that he was committing troops to the defense of Saudi Arabia and other allied nations in the Middle East. In that speech, Bush indicated that the US had "drawn a line in the sand" when it came to dealing with Saddam Hussein and his aggressive policies against neighboring countries. In this case, the president of the United States was signaling to the world that liberating Kuwait and protecting the Middle East had become a top priority, growing into a matter of national security.

In the years that followed the Gulf War, "drawing a line in the sand" would become one of Bush's most oft-quoted lines. As more and more people used the phrase, it soon joined the public lexicon, going from a simple reference to a famous presidential speech to symbolizing when a person had chosen to make a stand for something that they believed in. In other words, it has become a statement that is used when it is time to pick our battles and fight the fights that are important to us, both literally and figuratively.

So what exactly does it mean to choose your battles? Essentially, it is all about selecting the challenges, issues, and conflicts that personally mean the most to you, and deciding to direct your energy toward them. It is about determining what it worth taking a stand for and focusing your attention on those particular items. Conversely, it also means learning to let go of the things that don't mean as much, choosing to conserve your time and energy for other things instead.

On the surface, that may seem like something that is easy to do, but in reality, it can sometimes be surprisingly difficult. When it comes to picking our battles, we often find ourselves falling into one of two camps: those who are unwilling to take a stand for much of anything and those who are looking to take on every fight that comes their way. Both approaches can be incredibly unhealthy for us, but for very different reasons.

The person who never finds any battles worth fighting or simply doesn't want to stand up for themselves will often end up feeling isolated and

" Courage is what it takes to stand up and speak; courage is also what it takes to sit down and listen."

—Winston Churchill

There are several important things to consider when deciding which battles are worth turning our attention to, not the least of which is whether or not it is truly our battle to fight in the first place. It can be easy to get swept up in the causes of others by taking up the standard for someone who may not otherwise be able to fight for themselves. But in doing so we need to think about whether or not those individuals want or need us to speak on their behalf in the first place. Alternatively, we may also be bringing unwanted attention to a battle that they may not deem worth fighting. In doing so, we end up diverting our attention away from important matters that may be more worthy of our time and energy.

Knowing when to let others champion a cause that is more important to them is a vital skill to learn. Part of choosing your battles wisely is understanding that other people are doing the same and that there are times when we should just get out of the way and let them handle the fight themselves. This not only allows us to conserve our energy and attention for the things that mean the most to us personally, but it also gives others the opportunity to take center stage and pursue the fights that they have deemed important too.

That said, there are times when someone may indeed lack the ability, or the willingness, to stand up for the causes or topics that they believe in. In those cases it can be a very noble act to lend a hand, provided we have the ability to do so. Standing up for others who may not have a voice or platform of their own is a selfless act that can bring about positive results. Just keep in mind that you may not be able to devote all of the energy you need for your personal projects when you find yourself fighting battles for others. Learning to channel your time and energy toward the things that matter most is an important part of choosing your battles.

One key element that we all must understand when it comes to figuring out how to pick our battles wisely is that we simply don't have the resources to take on every fight. There will almost certainly be times when we want to do just that, but our time, energy, and insights are all limited, which is why we have to be strategic when it comes to deciding where to turn our attention. Beyond that, however, as previously mentioned, it simply isn't healthy for us to live in a constant state of conflict. If you do, you'll only find yourself mentally and physically exhausted, constantly distracted, and frequently on edge.

When it comes to choosing our battles, it is also good to remind ourselves that not everything is as important as it may first seem. Learning how to prioritize the things that mean the most to us is an essential skill that takes time to develop. Recognizing what things need to be addressed now, and which can be focused on later, requires time and introspection but can have an important payoff. Being able to rank those items from the most important to the least will play a big role in helping us decide exactly where we should channel our energies.

The ability to prioritize efficiently and effectively comes with time and experience, although exactly what our priorities are at any given time will shift throughout our lives. There will be occasions when success in our careers will be of the utmost importance, while family and friends may take center stage later. Being able to pick and choose where we want to divert our focus is crucial to planning which fights are worth taking on and which ones are best fought at another time.

There are a lot of variables to consider when weighing your priorities and trying to decide exactly what is important to you. For instance, you can ask yourself if the issue or project you are taking a stand on will have much of an impact on your life in a year or even five years down the road. How will it impact those around you? Will it help you in your career? Will it make your personal relationships stronger? Does it move you closer to your goals?

When it comes time to draw that proverbial line in the sand, you'll discover that some of the things that you hold dear will be on one side, while things that aren't so important are on the other. It is then that you'll start to understand which battles deserve your time and attention, and what things simply aren't worth fighting for.

Learning to prioritize is an important ability for any Navy SEAL to master. This is of course an indispensable skill to have on a battlefield, where split-second decisions can be the difference between success and failure. But SEALs begin honing their prioritization skills in the early days of their BUD/S (Basic Underwater Demolition/SEAL) training and it becomes an essential skill that is used throughout their career. Any SEAL candidate must learn to prioritize quickly if he hopes to earn his Special Warfare Insignia, more colloquially known as the SEAL Trident. This is the badge that is given upon the successful completion of BUD/S signifying that the wearer has joined the ranks of the SEAL teams.

BUD/S is notoriously difficult, however, with a high number of candidates washing out during the first phase alone. During that grueling seven-week program the SEAL trainees are pushed to their absolute limits, both mentally and physically, by running, swimming, and doing endless sets of push-ups, flutter kicks, and sit-ups. Many members of the class quit within the first half of Phase 1, in part because they can't compartmentalize and prioritize effectively.

Successful candidates learn early on that they have to set short term goals and stay focused on those objectives if they hope to make it through the training program. While some members of the class are constantly looking ahead to the next big challenge, which could be a few days or even a week down the road, others choose to set their milestones much closer. In fact, the trainees who seem to deal with the difficulties of BUD/S the best are the ones who break things down on a daily basis, prioritizing getting through the next four-mile soft-sand run or completing a two-mile swim rather than looking too far down the line. This allows them to manage those priorities more effectively and stay focused on their objectives, rather than getting overwhelmed with the bigger picture.

"

Who wishes to fight must first count the cost."

—Sun Tzu

This ability to set priorities continues to be an asset while working as part of a SEAL team after graduating from BUD/S as well. Learning to quickly and accurately identify the most important task at hand, and stay focused on accomplishing it, can prove to be vitally important while conducting a dangerous operation. But equally important is learning to recognize when those priorities may have shifted and having the flexibility to adjust to the changing conditions on the fly, allowing a SEAL and his team to think on their feet and remain flexible with their objectives.

Doggedly sticking to a set list of priorities can be just as dangerous for you as it is for a Navy SEAL, even if the consequences may not be quite so high. While it is certainly important to learn to prioritize when it comes to picking our battles, being able to change those priorities as needed is important too. It is not enough to identify the things that are most important to us at any given time, we must also recognize that those things can—and most likely will—shift in priority at various stages of our life.

Having established your priorities and decided where you want to draw your personal line in the sand, you'll gain a better sense of the things that mean the most to you. This will make it much easier to decide which battles you want to fight, although there are still plenty of other things to consider before doing so. For instance, it is important to think about whether or not this is a fight that you can truly win or if there are any consequences that could come with success or failure.

Choosing your battles wisely doesn't just involve being strategic with where you decide to take a stand, it usually means picking the fights that you have a chance of winning too. Fighting for a lost cause, while sometimes noble, can be emotionally and physically draining, leaving you feeling burned out and frustrated. Recognizing which battles are a long shot or are completely unwinnable can save you precious time and energy that can be devoted to other things. On the other hand, recognizing the fights that you most have a chance at winning makes it easier to decide where to channel your energy.

Defining what it means to "win" exactly will vary greatly depending on the circumstances. It could mean negotiating with your boss to allocate more funds for your departmental budget at the office or it could be convincing a friend to come around to your way of thinking on a hot social issue. A win could come in the form of something as significant as successfully standing up for the rights of others or it could be as simple as determining who gets to pick up the check at dinner. Being able to accurately assess the chances of scoring that win will play a role in whether or not you elect to fight a particular battle or save your strength for another day.

While picking the battles that we have the best chance of winning is a wise strategy, weighing the consequences of fighting that battle is worth considering too. If we choose to dig in and take a stand on a particular issue, will we end up alienating those around us? By winning that battle could we be harming our professional or personal relationships? Does a "win" now bring any potential complications or problems down the line? Are we being short-sighted in any way with the goals that we have set for ourselves? It is important that we avoid a Pyrrhic victory. That's a term that defines what happens when you technically are the victor in a battle, but it comes at such great cost that it negates any value that may have been gained by winning the fight in the first place. The term comes from King Pyrrhus of Epirus, who defeated Roman armies at the Battle of Heraclea and Battle of Asculum in 280 BC and 279 BC respectively. But in doing so, his forces incurred such heavy losses that it ultimately led to his retreat from the Italian peninsula even though he had his enemy on the run.

While Pyrrhus fought in actual life and death battles, we, too, can suffer Pyrrhic victories in the boardroom, office, and at home. For instance, it is possible to fight and win a civil court case, only to have legal fees end up costing more than what was awarded by the judge. Similarly, we could work long hours and sacrifice valuable time with friends and family to earn that promotion that we've been wanting, only to discover later that our success came at the loss of our health and irreparable damage to our relationships. On paper, we won the battle, but at what cost?

Worse yet, what if we end up losing the battle? Even when we think we're choosing the right fight to focus our attention on, no outcome is ever assured. We may take a stand on an issue that is very important to us, only to still end up not achieving what we set out to do. Could that have a lasting impact on our relationships as well? Could it put our careers in jeopardy? Does taking a stand—and losing—end up diminishing our standing with those we work or share a home with?

Both winning and losing can bring consequences, and it pays to consider what those consequences could be. Understanding the risks involved with pursuing the things that you care about the most will not only help you decide which battles are worth fighting, but they'll help you plot your strategies for fighting them too. Armed with that knowledge, you can also avoid potential pitfalls and landmines that could throw off your plans and make life more difficult in the long run.

All of that said, there are times when it may be necessary to fight a battle that isn't necessarily going to end in victory. You may come across an issue that seems like a lost cause, but it is still worth taking a stand on simply because it is the right thing to do. Calling out social injustices or illegal activity in the workplace can be a no-win situation, leading to alienation from coworkers, getting ostracized by supervisors, or even termination. Those types of battles are not ones that are easy to take up, often requiring a great deal of courage in the face of overwhelming odds and potentially devastating outcomes.

"

Don't fight a battle if you don't gain anything by winning."

—Erwin Rommel

An example of this is Tyler Schultz, the grandson of former secretary of state George Schultz. Tyler once worked for the now-defunct and disgraced medical testing company Theranos, for which his grandfather served on the board of directors. While there, the younger Schultz witnessed fraudulent and potentially dangerous activity, which would eventually put him at odds, not only with Theranos executives but important members of his family too.

Founded in 2003 by a charismatic and ambitious Stanford dropout named Elizabeth Holmes, Theranos promised to revolutionize the health care industry. Holmes claimed to have developed a device called the Edison that could perform dozens of medical tests using just a single drop of blood, eliminating the need to take large blood samples and potentially saving patients thousands of dollars in the process.

The problem was, the Edison didn't really work as advertised, despite the fact that Theranos had raised hundreds of millions of dollars from investors and spent years trying to develop the device. The technology inside the machine was capable of running just a handful of tests, which was far fewer than what Holmes said it could do. Worse yet, those tests were often wildly inaccurate, putting the health of patients at risk.

In 2013, Tyler Schultz's influential grandfather pulled some strings and landed him a job at Theranos. The young man was excited to work for a company that was on the cutting edge of technology and was striving to change the medical industry. It wasn't long before he started to see discrepancies between what Holmes told the media and investors versus what was really happening inside the company. This soon set off alarms in the mind of the recent college graduate.

The fact of the matter was, Theranos technicians often used devices built by the competition to perform its medical tests simply because they were faster, more accurate, and more dependable than the Edison. Of course, that was a tightly-controlled secret that could have sunk the company had it gone public, so Holmes and other executives worked hard to avoid that information getting out.

In April of 2014, just eight months after he started at Theranos, Tyler sent an email to Elizabeth

Holmes detailing the issues that he had witnessed in the lab, which included faulty Edison machines and inaccurate tests. His hope was to raise awareness about those problems with the CEO in hopes of getting her to examine the practices in the lab more closely. At the time, Schultz still believed in what Theranos was doing and thought that he was taking a stand for something that truly mattered.

Holmes later sent an email back to Schultz informing him that she would have her team look into the faulty devices and poor test results. What she did instead was forward Tyler's email on to Theranos President and CEO, Ramesh "Sunny" Balwani, who took the young man to task for questioning the company's procedures. Schultz was told in no uncertain terms that Bulwani and Holmes expected a full apology from him and that he should ask no further questions.

The handling of that email convinced Tyler more than ever that something was seriously wrong at Theranos. So, he quit his job that day and met with his grandfather to discuss the situation. The elder Schultz listened intently while his grandson recounted tales of Holmes and other executives suppressing internal inquiries from employees regarding the accuracy of the Edison device and its ability to run blood tests. When he was finished speaking, Tyler's grandfather looked at him intently, told him that he respected his opinion, but in this case the young man was simply wrong. George Schultz believed in Elizabeth Holmes completely and was sure that she was on the brink of revolutionizing health care as we know it.

Tyler walked away from that meeting convinced that he had to do something, not just for the patients that were relying on Theranos for their health exams, but to protect his grandfather's reputation too. He started that process by first reaching out to state regulators in California and New York, prompting them to investigate what was happening inside Theranos. He also secretly began speaking with John Carreyrou, a journalist at the *Wall Street Journal,* and began telling him the story too. The writer had reached out to Tyler weeks earlier over the internet, but initially Schultz had ignored Carreyrou's overtures. Later, he responded to those messages, eventually sparking a damning article that would result in the downfall of Holmes and

Theranos. Before that happened, however, Schultz was faced with more difficult choices and challenges.

Theranos executives eventually got wind that Schultz was speaking to the press and accused him of violating a nondisclosure agreement he signed when he became an employee. They warned him in no uncertain terms that legal action could be forthcoming if he continued to talk to Carreyrou and pressured him to reveal the other sources that the writer was in contact with.

Tyler held his ground, despite his parents and grandfather putting enormous pressure on him to walk away from the entire Theranos situation. George Schultz remained a member of the company's board of directors and was convinced that Elizabeth Holmes and her team of technicians were making enormous strides toward changing medicine and health care in the US. For the older Schultz it was unfathomable that anything was amiss.

At one point, George invited Tyler over to his house to discuss the matter, hoping to resolve the tension that had come between them. But when his grandson arrived, he was surprised to find two Theranos lawyers waiting for him. They attempted to pressure the young man into signing documents that they said would make everything go away, but he again refused to comply. Deep down, he knew that he was doing the right thing, even if his family couldn't see it at the time.

In the months that followed, a rift formed between grandfather and grandson, with the two rarely speaking to one another. Tyler even skipped George's 95th birthday party as the two continued to butt heads over their opposing views of Theranos. By that time, the company had begun legal proceedings in an attempt to silence Tyler, who would eventually rack up more than $400,000 in attorney fees fighting Holmes and her lawyers in court.

"

Pick battles big enough
to matter, small enough
to win."

—Jonathan Kozol

In October of 2015, Carreyrou published the first of several scathing articles about Theranos in the *Wall Street Journal*. Using much of what he had learned from Tyler—and other informants—he began to peel back the layers of fraud and deception that Holmes had perpetrated while running the company.

The story detailed the ongoing issues with the Edison machine and the great lengths that Holmes and her team went through to keep its deficiencies from coming out. Carreyrou's article began the process of systematically unraveling Theranos's carefully crafted narrative, which ran counter to everything that Tyler had seen while he was working there. This wasn't a company that was looking to change modern medicine, but was instead deceiving investors and patients about the capabilities of its technology. It was fraud on the highest level, with people's lives and health hanging in the balance.

An investigation conducted by the US Securities and Exchange Commission revealed "elaborate, years-long fraud" on the part of Elizabeth Holmes and members of her team. Later she would be indicted on charges of wire fraud and conspiracy, settling out of court for $500,000 without admitting any wrongdoing. That would spell the end of the company she created, which closed its doors for good in late 2018.

Although it took some time, Tyler Schultz was eventually fully vindicated. The claims he made against Theranos all proved to be true, and his decision to stand up for what he believed was right played an instrumental role in the company's downfall. Despite intense pressure from Theranos's attorneys and charismatic CEO—not to mention his famous grandfather—Tyler stayed committed to getting the true story out. In the end, his courage kept potential investors from losing hundreds of millions of dollars while also keeping thousands of innocent people safe from dangerously inaccurate medical tests.

At some point throughout the ordeal there were probably times when Tyler Schultz felt as if he was in a battle that he couldn't win. Theranos had deep pockets, a team of high-priced lawyers, and a media-savvy CEO, all of which were being used to call into question his honesty and credibility. Despite all of those challenges he still chose to fight that battle because it was the right thing to do.

Having the courage and conviction to fight a battle that appears hopeless from the outset isn't easy. Most of the time, those are exactly the kind of fights we want to avoid, although sometimes we have to take a stand for what's right too. In the case of Tyler Schultz, his fight against Theranos ended up costing him dearly. Not only did he lose his job, but his unwillingness to settle out of court left him estranged from his grandfather, and squarely at the center of one of the biggest cases of corporate fraud in US history. Fortunately, in the end, his story proved to be accurate, allowing him to overcome the Theranos propaganda machine and rebuild his relationship with his grandfather.

Which brings us to another important thing to consider when it comes to choosing our battles. Before deciding one way or another, ask yourself how you would feel if you chose *not* to take a stand on a certain subject or cause. If you didn't draw a line in the sand over a specific topic, would anyone else? And if that particular battle isn't fought, what kind of lasting impact will it have on your life?

Thinking strategically, and engaging in the fights that count, is what choosing your battles wisely is all about. If you determine that the battle would have a minimal impact, then it is probably a clear indicator that it isn't worth fighting. If that's the case, save your time and energy for something more important.

On the other hand, if you take everything into account and determine that a certain battle could have a very real and lasting impact on your life or that of those around you, then it is probably something that you do want to take a stand on. Those are the kinds of struggles that are generally worth fighting for and have the most potential for creating positive change, not only on ourselves but for others too.

In the case of Tyler Schultz, had he decided to just walk away from Theranos and not taken a stand against the rampant fraud that he saw there, it still seems likely that blood testing scam would have eventually come to light anyway. That doesn't mean that it wasn't something that he needed to address. Schultz's actions likely saved millions of dollars for other investors, but beyond that it may have actually saved the lives of some patients. Simply put, it was a battle he couldn't ignore, because it would have been tough to live with the consequences had more people been hurt.

Hopefully most of us will never find ourselves facing that kind of decision. For us, choosing our battles wisely will probably come down to making choices that have a more direct impact on our lives rather than those of tens of thousands of other people. Still, the question remains the same; if we don't fight a particular battle, what will the result be and are we able to accept those outcomes?

Learning to pick your battles wisely is a skillset that is developed with time. With experience we learn that sometimes being strategic with where we draw our personal line in the sand can end up having a bigger impact than if we fought a hundred smaller battles that have less value or meaning. That is the power of choosing wisely, as it conveys a sense of *gravitas* that is often lost when you try to fight multiple battles at the same time.

It is also important to always keep in mind that wisdom comes from making mistakes, and chances are you'll choose the wrong battles on occasion.

If that happens, don't dwell on those setbacks for long. Instead, learn from them, regroup, and move on. Take the knowledge that you've gained and use it in the future, allowing it to serve as a guide for use in all of those potential battles yet to come.

66

The quality of a person's life is in direct propor- tion to their commitment to excellence, regardless of their chosen field of endeavor."

—Vince Lombardi

PART II

FIGHT THE GOOD FIGHT

In late 2010, US intelligence officers received compelling evidence that a high-value target was holed up in a fortified compound located in the Pakistani city of Abbottabad. At the time, they weren't exactly sure who the high-ranking Al-Qaeda member was, but there were some indications that it could be Osama bin Laden. Almost ten years earlier, bin Laden had masterminded the attacks on the World Trade Center in New York City on 9/11, which quickly made him the most wanted man on the planet and forced him to go into hiding.

For years the Central Intelligence Agency, National Security Agency, US Department of Defense, and numerous other organizations had tirelessly followed every credible lead in their hunt to find the terrorist leader. His trail had gone cold after the US invasion of Afghanistan in December of 2001, although from time to time they would receive a tip on his possible whereabouts. None of those leads ever panned out, however, and more than nine years after the attacks on the Twin Towers, bin Laden remained at large.

Ultimately it was a combination of electronic surveillance, satellite imagery, drone flights, and other high tech tools that uncovered where bin Laden had been hiding. US intelligence officers spent countless hours analyzing the data that was collected, looking for signs of who might be hiding inside the unusual compound in Abbottabad. Over time they became convinced that someone of importance to the Al-Qaeda organization was located there, with some even speculating that it was bin Laden himself.

That was enough for President Barack Obama to officially authorize Operation Neptune Spear in April of 2011 and for members of SEAL Team Six to conduct a daring raid on the compound on May 2 of that same year. That was the mission that led to the death of Osama bin Laden, bringing an end to one of the longest and most intense manhunts in human history.

The operation is a good example of Obama and his military advisors choosing their battles wisely. It was a high-risk, high-reward mission that could have had disastrous consequences from both a military and diplomatic standpoint. But after considering all of the variables and examining the potential outcomes, the president and his men knew that they couldn't let this opportunity pass by. It was a literal and figurative battle that needed to be fought to send a message to both Al-Qaeda operatives and American citizens alike.

Once President Obama approved moving ahead with Operation Neptune Spear, the Navy SEALs who eventually conducted the raid began preparing for the mission. To help them get as prepared as possible, a replica of bin Laden's compound was built in a secret location in North Carolina. The SEALs conducted daily drills within that model, studying every square inch of the place so that when they arrived at the real thing, they had a good understanding of its floor plan and the location of the exits. While at the training facility, they also devised and prepared for countless contingencies, hoping to account for as many variables as possible prior to setting off to their staging ground in Afghanistan.

All of that preparation and training proved to be incredibly valuable once the mission was officially underway. When the actual raid took place, every man on the team knew exactly what his role was and where he should be at any given time while sweeping through the compound. As a result, the operation went off with extreme precision, even after a top-secret stealth helicopter crashed while inserting the SEALs into bin Laden's stronghold. As part of their preparation, the team had even planned for the possibility of losing one of the aircraft, so none of the men were particularly phased when the helicopter went down.

There is a popular motto amongst Navy SEALs that says, "The more sweat and tears you shed in training, the less blood you shed in combat." The members of the team that assaulted the compound in Abbottabad took that mantra to heart, spending countless hours preparing for the raid so that everything would go off as close to as planned as possible. Their intense training and preparation gave them the best chance of not only pulling off the daring mission but coming home in one piece as well. In other words, they were ready to fight the fight that was necessary to complete their objective.

Unlike most people, SEALs rarely have the luxury of picking and choosing their battles. Usually they are called upon to do a job that has been selected for them, with little room for error, and none for failure. Those battles may be chosen by someone at a higher pay grade, but nevertheless, the SEALs are the instruments used to fight them. That means they have to be ready to face whatever challenges are put in front of them and pursue their objectives in an efficient and professional manner.

Once we've decided exactly where to take a stand, we have to prepare for the very real possibility that a fight could follow. Usually when we choose our battles there is generally something of personal importance at stake, which means someone could have an opposing view or opinion that runs counter to our own. When that happens, we should be ready to face them on the battlefield, which for most of us means confronting them in the boardroom, on the athletic field, at a committee meeting, or wherever else we've decided to make our stand.

Just as the SEALs approach their jobs with a high degree of professionalism, it is important that you do the same when seeking to resolve conflicts in your life. The battles that we choose to fight often involve issues, challenges, and topics that we're highly passionate about, which can cause us to say things we don't necessarily mean or lash out in ways that are heated and personal. When wading into the fight, try to keep in mind that the other person may feel just as strongly about the subject too. This can lead to disagreements or even strained relationships, which at the end of the day may end up causing difficulties at a future date, sometimes long after the conflict has been resolved.

66

Never be afraid to stand with the minority when the minority is right, for the minority that is right will one day be the majority."

—William Jennings Bryan

Before taking up the fight it is also important to assess what your objectives are. If your goal is to defend your point of view, champion the cause of others, or stand up for something important to you, then you're probably on the right track. On the other hand, if you're fighting the battle simply because you want to stand in the way of others, cause harm, or to be vindictive in some way, then you're fighting for all of the wrong reasons. At that point, you probably need to take a step back and reassess the situation. Chances are you're on a course that could do irreparable harm on a personal or professional level.

When SEALs are sent off on a mission they are usually given very clearly defined rules of engagement (ROEs). Those rules are a set of directives that dictate just when, where, how, and with whom the team can initiate combat, use lethal force, and so on. These parameters can be restrictive at times, but they are meant to help maintain a sense of order and discipline, defining how to interact with civilians, enemy hostiles, prisoners, and so on. The ROEs are also created to help the SEALs stay within the strategic, political, and legal bounds of the operation.

We should learn to develop our own rules of engagement when it comes to fighting our battles. Those rules can serve as a personal code of conduct, ensuring that we interact with others in a professional and respectful manner, even while taking a stand on the things that matter to us the most. This can help us avoid causing serious damage to our relationships with coworkers, friends, and family, while engaging in intelligent and constructive dialogs.

Our ROEs should include things like staying open to other people's ideas and perspectives, actively listening to their point of view, and giving them ample time to voice their concerns. In doing so, we're much more likely to have them return the favor, keeping the conversation more civil and productive as a result.

We should also strive to maintain our composure at all times and avoid saying things out of spite or anger. Even if the conversation gets heated, don't lash out or resort to name-calling. Always keep in mind that the person you are engaging with is quite possibly someone you'll have to maintain a relationship with in the future, too. It is important to avoid actions or words that you could end up regretting down the line.

From time to time, it's helpful to remind ourselves that the individuals whom we are interacting with are not the enemy; they are simply on the other side of an issue or topic that we've both chosen to take a stand on. At the end of the day, we should still be able to maintain a high level of respect for one another, even if we disagree on some topics. By maintaining an open dialog, remaining professional and polite, and avoiding personal attacks, we can usually avoid burning bridges that could come back to haunt us later.

When defining your personal rules of engagement, always remember to focus directly on the problem or issue that is at the center of the fight, but don't attack the person you may be at odds with. Be ready to present clear, well-thought-out solutions to the challenges that you face, and focus more on making decisions rather than creating obstacles. Avoid placing blame or pointing fingers at others as that is counterproductive behavior that can lead to strained relationships, bruised feelings, and longstanding grudges.

The rules of engagement that we set for ourselves should never include the use of ultimatums either. Attempting to use an ultimatum to get our way may result in the outcome that you want, but it can also lead to resentment, frustration, and anger. Worse yet, if someone calls you on that ultimatum and things don't go your way, you have to be prepared to back up your threats or end up looking indecisive or disingenuous. It could also cast a dark cloud over future interactions where any further use of ultimatums could be truly devastating to the trust of the individuals who are involved.

Finally, be prepared to face defeat. We may have learned to pick our battles wisely, but that doesn't mean we're going to win them all. If a choice is made that goes against our beliefs and feelings, sometimes all we can do is concede to that outcome and move on to fight another day. When this occurs we may be given the opportunity to weigh in on the decision, offer our advice and opinion, or even make a case explaining why we disagree with the final outcome. Where things go from there isn't always under our control and it is better to acknowledge that and learn to move on rather than continuing to fight for a lost cause.

This commonly happens in a workplace environment. For example, we might have strong feelings about a particular direction or decision that our company or organization has made. We might choose to voice our opinion and offer our thoughts on such decisions and even make suggestions on a course of action that we think might work out better. But if a boss or supervisor chooses to go a different way there is little we can do about it other than accept that decision. Sometimes it is in our best interest to cut our losses and move on, even when waging a battle over something that we care deeply about.

With your ROEs established, you'll have a solid platform for how to handle yourself during just about any type of conflict. Whether you're debating with friends over a hot button political issue, having a heart-to-heart talk with a significant other, or searching for viable business solutions with co-workers, conducting yourself with class, dignity, and professionalism can go a very long way. Part of fighting the good fight is avoiding leaving a swath of emotional and mental destruction in your wake.

One of the ways you can do that is to seek solutions that are beneficial to all parties involved. When it comes to conflict resolution, classic game theorists and economists will tell us there are typically three types of outcomes—zero-sum games, negative-sum games, and positive-sum games. In other words, most conflicts either end up with one side winning and the other losing, both sides losing, or both sides winning. The hope is that we can strive to find solutions that are good for everyone involved, although that isn't always possible.

If we approach any conflict as a zero-sum game and we win and the opposing side loses, what defines a "win" or "loss" is going to vary greatly from situation to situation. For instance, sporting events are almost always zero-sum games, with one team winning and the other losing. In a business environment, two departments could be vying for the same slice of the budget that allows them to pursue a specific project. If one gets the money and the other doesn't, it is a zero-sum outcome. Similarly, if you and a friend have both applied for a job, only one of you can get it, which is also a zero sum-scenario.

"

An eye for an eye only
makes the whole world
blind."

—Mahatma Gandhi

negative-sum game means that both parties in a given conflict end up losing. This can happen in a military engagement. For example, both sides can inflict so much damage to one another that neither of them can claim victory. This can also happen in a professional setting where an economic downturn causes budget cuts, which end up impacting everyone. With fewer funds to go around it, is possible that no one will be able to maintain their current economic position.

A positive-sum game is one in which everyone gains something in the end. In order to do that, both sides of a conflict or negotiation must find a way to cooperate so that all of the participants benefit. That isn't to say that the gains achieved by both sides are of the same level, but no one walks away with having lost anything either.

An example of a positive-sum game could be two departments in the same office sharing a budget surplus. If just one of the departments is given the funds they are allowed to pursue their goals, while the other one must simply do without. But by sharing the money, both sides are able to make progress toward their objectives, even if they don't have enough cash to achieve their loftiest ambitions.

Creating a positive-sum resolution is almost always the optimal outcome, but it is also the most difficult to achieve. In order to do that both sides of any conflict have to be willing to work together to resolve the situation in a way that benefits everyone involved. The downside is that such an agreement rarely results in an overwhelming win for either party, but no one walks away from the negotiating table as a loser either.

Sometimes achieving a win-win situation is impossible, as not every standoff can be resolved in a way that results in a positive-sum. In fact, the majority of conflicts end up falling into the zero-sum category, where one side scores a win more or less at the expense of the other. This is often the case when there are limited resources to go around and only one of the sides can actually obtain them. It is also a common outcome when a decision is being made between two opposing viewpoints or competing plans where one option is simply chosen over the other. In those cases, a choice has to be made on which direction to go, and one side or the other is naturally going to end up on the losing end.

Regardless of which side of that decision you end up on, it is important to remind ourselves about the ROEs that we've created for ourselves. If you remain both a gracious winner or loser it will help you maintain your relationships and ensure that they continue moving forward in an amicable fashion. Be respectful, empathetic, and supportive of those on the opposite side. Chances are, you'll be in their position at one point or another and will appreciate the same consideration being shown for your point of view as well.

For obvious reasons, we should go to great lengths to avoid a negative-sum outcome whenever possible. If the result of a standoff or conflict ends up with both sides losing, the results can be potentially very damaging. Typically speaking, the fallout from such a situation can lead to hard feelings, distrust, resentment, and anger. It can also cloud future negotiations and interactions with the individuals involved, creating roadblocks to collaboration.

Most of the time people will do whatever it takes to avoid a negative-sum game simply because in the long run it ends up penalizing everyone involved. That's not a winning strategy in any kind of conflict and ends up being extremely counterproductive in the long run. The exception to this rule is if one of the parties involved in the dispute is willing to accept the loss that they will take just to prevent the other side from winning. That is an unreasonable and spiteful approach to have, but in some cases it is a real possibility.

A famous example of this is the intense rivalry that developed between Ford Motors and Italian sports car manufacturer Ferrari back in the early 1960s. Fueled by the intense egos running both companies, the two automobile legends would end up spending millions of dollars in an arms race that would play out on race tracks all over the world, often putting the lives of drivers in danger in the process.

The rivalry began in 1963 when Henry Ford II negotiated a deal to purchase the Italian company from its enigmatic founder Enzo Ferrari. Ford thought that the acquisition would bring his company increased credibility with sports car enthusiasts and provide a leg up in auto racing too. At that time,

Ferrari dominated the motorsport scene, routinely winning some of the biggest races in the world.

The deal was essentially agreed upon in principle and company executives from Ford flew to Italy to sign the final contracts. But at the last minute, Enzo elected to pull out of the deal altogether, refusing to sell to his American rival. Feeling like a jilted bride, Ford was incensed by Ferrari's last-minute change of heart and vowed to beat him on the biggest stage in racing—the 24 Hours of Le Mans.

First held in 1923, Le Mans quickly grew into the crown jewel of automobile racing. Run on a mix of roads and race tracks, the event is not only a test of speed but of endurance. Both the driver and the car must run for twenty-four hours straight, forcing manufacturers to not only concentrate on how fast they could make their vehicles, but also how reliable and fuel-efficient they could be.

To underscore just how dominant Ferrari was at the time, the company didn't lose a single race at Le Mans between 1960 and 1965. So when Henry Ford II vowed to dethrone the Italian legend, he knew it would be an uphill battle from the start. At that time, the American car manufacturer had no significant racing legacy to speak of, which made the very idea of Ford beating Ferrari on the track seem ludicrous.

"

Better to fight for something than live for nothing."

—George S. Patton

But Ford was a man who not only felt scorned, he also happened to have very deep pockets. Following the failed deal with Ferrari, he returned home to Detroit and immediately ordered the creation of his own sports car that could go head-to-head with anything the Italians produced. To accomplish this he let it be known that money was no object and hired some of the best designers in the automotive industry, including the legendary Carroll Shelby, a man who was known for creating fast, high-performance sports cars unlike anything else on the market.

Over the next two years, Ford focused on developing a super car that could hold its own at Le Mans, eventually creating the now-iconic GT40. At first, the vehicle, although fast and powerful, was unreliable and problematic, providing mixed results on the track. As a result, the car would deliver both spectacular wins and utter disappointments.

In 1964, Ford took three cars to Le Mans in hopes of dethroning Ferrari, but all three models retired early, unable to finish the race. The following year, the GT40 came back for another go, but once again mechanical breakdowns prevented it from seriously contending. Meanwhile, Ferrari went on to win its sixth consecutive title and looked practically unstoppable on the endurance racing circuit.

Ford was more determined than ever to put the upstart Italian company in its place, entering the 1966 racing season with renewed confidence. The previous two years had provided plenty of expensive—but valuable—lessons to Shelby and his team of engineers. Despite the fact that they had yet to win at Le Mans, they were continually making subtle and important changes to the car, improving reliability and performance in some very significant ways. The GT40 had shown glimpses of its capabilities in the past, but Ford and the entire racing team were eager to show off to the international racing community what it could really do.

The 1966 season began with a dominant showing in Daytona, where the GT40 not only won the event, but Ford's three cars finished first, second, and third in the standings. The team followed that up with the same result, taking the three podium spots at the 12 Hours of Sebring race too. That left just Le Mans, and another showdown with archrival Ferrari, on the calendar.

By the time the 24 Hours of Le Mans came around in June, Enzo Ferrari was well-aware that the American company had made huge strides in designs and reliability with the GT40. He knew that he couldn't just sit on his laurels, so he ordered his racing team to come up with ways to improve their vehicles as well. The result was the 330 P3, a model that was shorter and wider than the previous generation race car, that also cranked out more horsepower.

Several other manufacturers brought new cars to Le Mans that year, including Porsche, Chevrolet, and Matra, but most fans knew this was a showdown between incumbent champion Ferrari and a very focused and determined Ford team. The public spat between Enzo and Henry Ford II was common knowledge with racing fans, and that bad-blood was playing out on the biggest and most prestigious stage that the sport had to offer. In the end, it was a battle that wasn't even close. After three years of designing and building the ultimate endurance race car, Ford finally broke through, leaving every other competitor—Ferrari included—in the dust. In fact, the American company's win was so dominant, that the GT40 team once again finished first, second, and third, making it a clean sweep for the Grand Slam of endurance racing that year.

Although Henry Ford II had accomplished what he had promised to do, beating Ferrari at Le Mans once simply wasn't enough. His racing team would go on to win the next three years as well, putting together an unprecedented string of victories for an American car manufacturer at the event. From 1966–1969, the GT40 turned back all competitors, earning itself a spot amongst the most iconic race cars ever built.

What Ford accomplished with the GT40 is nothing short of remarkable. Essentially, the company went from having no experience in the endurance racing arena to winning its highest-profile events in just three years. Most of the other competitors in the race had been designing cars for Le Mans for decades, and arch-rival Ferrari had won the previous six races. It was a stunning achievement for Henry Ford II in particular, who may not have even embarked on his quest had Enzo Ferrari agreed to sell his company in the first place.

After being jilted by the Italian automaker, Ford launched a personal crusade to beat Ferrari at Le Mans. In the process, he started an automotive war of sorts that had both companies spending vast sums of cash to battle one another out on the track. For the American company that meant designing and building a new sports car from the ground up, spending millions of dollars in the process. Ferrari, on the other hand, didn't have as deep of pockets as his nemesis, but he, too, was forced to spend vast sums of cash. First to fend off his foe, and then later to try to play catch-up after his company was dethroned at Le Mans.

It would be easy to look at this story and see it as a zero-sum game. After all, Ford gained his revenge by besting his opponent on the track just as he had promised he would. But taking a step back and looking at it from a different perspective, it could be interpreted as a negative-sum game too. Both sides ended up spending millions of dollars fighting against one another with little more to show for it than a trophy. Yes, winning at Les Mans brings a high level of prestige, and the research and development that was done for the cars eventually trickled down to consumer models. But for the most part, neither Ford nor Ferrari truly recouped the money they spent battling one another.

The cost of the Ford-Ferrari rivalry can't simply be boiled down to the amount of money they spent either. Several of the drivers lost their lives while testing and racing the sports cars that the two companies created. That included celebrated racer Ken Miles, who was a loyal member of the Ford team. He lost his life just two months after that first historic win at Les Mans while testing a prototype of the next version of the GT40.

"

You won't always win
your battles, but it's good
to know you fought."

—Lauren Bacall

The Ford vs. Ferrari story is dramatic and interesting, but it is also a byproduct of the collision of two massive personalities. At the end of the day, Enzo Ferrari decided that he didn't want to relinquish control of his company and the racing team he had built. For his part, Henry Ford II wasn't accustomed to anyone telling him no, so he took it as a personal insult when the Italian automaker backed out of the deal. The clash that followed makes for an entertaining footnote in racing history, but it could have been completely avoided had either of the two men not allowed their egos to get involved.

That is an important lesson for us to keep in mind. After we've chosen our battles and stepped up to the fight, don't allow your ego to dictate your ROE or cloud your judgment on when it is time to walk away. Pushing a conflict out of spite and having an unwillingness to back down, even after recognizing that the battle is over, can be detrimental to both personal and professional relationships. It can also cloud your decision making and cause you to lose sight of your original objectives.

When it comes to fighting your battles it is always important to keep your eyes on the prize. Whether your objective is to convince your boss to pursue an important deal or hold your ground on an important topic or social issue, it pays to stay focused on what it is you hope to achieve. Getting sidetracked can cause you to spend precious resources and time on things that don't matter, keeping you from making progress toward your goal.

Once again, the rules of engagement that you've created for yourself can serve as a guide. By avoiding making personal attacks, and staying respectful of your opponent at all times, we can learn to keep our egos in check. As a result, we can use our time and energy more efficiently and avoid getting caught up in unnecessary squabbles that serve no other purpose but to distract us from our true mission.

Despite the fact that they are amongst the most well-trained and efficient warriors on the planet, most Navy SEALs learn early on to check their egos at the door. That's because they know that in order to be successful they need to work together as a team. Each man brings a unique set of skills and talents that make him a formidable opponent in his own right. But when a group of such extraordinary individuals is able to set aside their ego and work together, they can accomplish amazing things.

Many of the candidates that enter BUD/S training come in with a high level of confidence in their abilities. Most of them are already exceptional athletes who are in great physical condition. They also tend to be smart, driven individuals who have been successful throughout their young lives, both athletically and academically. However, during their training they're pushed to their absolute physical and mental limits, forcing them to reevaluate their own strengths and weaknesses.

When faced with uncertainty and doubt for the first time, many of the SEAL trainees find that their confidence has been shaken to its core. This often occurs when they come up against a challenge unlike any that they've ever faced before. The candidates who can set aside their ego, create a tough mindset, and can remain focused on their goal will have a much better shot of making it through to BUD/S graduation. Those who can't will almost assuredly wash out.

Navy SEALs are often described as the "quiet professionals," a moniker they've earned due to the fact that they tend to go about their jobs without seeking fame or adulation. Instead, they take on some of the most difficult missions the US military has to offer, usually without public acknowledgment of any kind. In order to do that, they have to completely let go of their ego and replace it with a deep sense of duty to the causes they are fighting for. They also create a strong and lasting connection with the other members of their elite brotherhood. Letting one of those brothers in arms down in the thick of an intense situation is unacceptable, which only further demonstrates their lack of ego.

When Navy SEALs are pressed into action they do so with a clearly defined plan. The operation will always have a set of objectives in mind and the goals will always be clearly spelled out before the team is deployed. This not only helps the SEALs to stay on task, but it also helps them to understand when the mission is over and evaluate whether or not it was a success.

Over the course of the mission, that plan may shift in scope or have its objectives redefined based on what happens in the field. A SEAL's training allows him to be highly adaptable, giving him the flexibility needed to deal with contingencies as the need arises. Few operations ever go exactly to plan, but thanks to his training, a SEAL can roll with the unexpected while remaining focused on the mission.

After we draw a line in the sand signifying the battles that we've chosen to fight, it is a good idea for us to take a similar approach. Before engaging in conflict, it is important to ask ourselves what our endgame is exactly. What do we hope to accomplish by taking a stand on this particular topic and how will we know if we've been successful?

Those may seem like questions that are easy to answer, and in some cases they very well may be. Nevertheless, it is important to take some time to consider them prior to making our stand. Being able to define what our objectives are will serve as the starting point for developing our personal battle plan, which will end up serving as our guide throughout the conflict.

By first asking ourselves what it is we want to accomplish we're creating the goals that we hope to achieve by taking on this particular battle. Our objective could be something as simple as just wanting to have our opinion heard on a specific topic or it could have a far greater impact on our professional and personal life. Depending on the nature and size of that topic, it could even have far-reaching implications for the lives of others too.

"

Don't find fault,
find a remedy."

—Henry Ford

Defining our objectives at the start gives us a clear target to aim for at all times. Once again, this can help us stay on track and prevent us from getting bogged down with things that don't truly matter. It will allow us to understand whether or not we're making progress and if we ultimately achieve what we set out to do.

Beyond just defining what it is we hope to accomplish, it helps to come armed with potential solutions too. Electing to take a stand on a particular issue or problem is one thing, but coming up with realistic solutions is an entirely different matter. Anyone can point fingers at where things need to be improved or refined, but the people who truly get things done are those who already have a plan of action in mind. If you have a complaint, always voice the complaint with a solution or at least options for others to consider. It is far easier to get others on board with the plan if you've already thought through how to solve the problem.

Having a clearly defined solution is integral to creating our battle plan, which is essentially the course of action that we'll follow in order to achieve our objectives and goals. Usually the plan consists of a set of steps or micro-goals that serve as the road map to reaching our objectives. Sometimes the plan provides plenty of details, such as when you're proposing an important shift in the way your company manages its personnel and resources. Other times the battle plan is more nebulous, as when you're debating a friend about a political topic or some type of social issue.

One of the key points of any battle plan is defining an exit strategy and deciding exactly where your exit point lies. Essentially, that's the point in any debate or conflict where you decide that it's time to move on, regardless of the outcome. Recognizing exactly when to pull the plug can save you a lot of frustration in the long run, particularly when a certain fight continues to drag on.

How exactly you define your exit point is completely up to you and can be based on a number of different variables. For instance, it could occur when you're simply too exhausted to continue fighting or when you've run out of time to dedicate to the cause. Alternatively, it could occur when you've passed a predefined deadline, which brings an end to the conflict simply because there is no longer any reason to continue. Depending on the nature of the fight you may decide to stick it out long enough to have had a chance to say your peace, or stick it out until the very end, no matter the costs and consequences.

If you find yourself embroiled in a conflict but don't have a well-defined battle plan or clear exit strategy, you run the risk of getting bogged down. It's possible you could find yourself burning valuable time and energy on a fight that will end up costing you more than you could possibly ever get back out of it. When that happens you have to be able to not just recognize that fact but be prepared to extricate yourself from the situation by any means possible. If you can't, you may find yourself in a never-ending cycle that prevents you from pursuing other important objectives.

When considering where our exit point sits, it often helps to do a cost-benefit analysis. In this case, we have to consider the cost—in terms of effort, time, money, etc.—that a drawn-out fight could accrue versus the benefits we get out of it in return. When those costs increase to a point that they are higher in value than the benefits that are gained, it is a clear sign that it is time to start channeling your resources elsewhere.

No doubt there will be times when we are approaching that exit point but we'll still want to continue the fight. In learning to choose our battles wisely, we're naturally picking issues and projects that hold deep meaning for us. Because of this, we'll also tend to have more invested in those conflicts, which in turn can make us more reluctant to give up even when our instincts are telling us we should move on.

It is important to keep in mind that choosing to exit a fight doesn't mean that you're giving up or even actually losing the battle. It simply means that you've very wisely chosen to avoid wasting more time and energy on a conflict that has no resolution in sight and is proving to be a bigger quagmire than originally expected. It is one thing to commit yourself to a battle that you feel is worth fighting, but it is entirely a different matter to have that fight continue on well past a reasonable expiration date.

Continuing to push a battle for longer than it needs to be fought can create lasting repercussions that could cloud our relationships or lead to potential clashes in the future. Holding our ground on a position that we feel is right is a noble endeavor, but so is knowing when to let go and move on to more collaborative options. If we're unable to find a way to do that, our showdowns can lead to long and lasting grudges, hurt feelings, and intense rivalries that could force us to miss out on rewarding opportunities in the future.

One of the most famous rivalries in modern business took place between Microsoft co-founder Bill Gates and Apple co-founder Steve Jobs. Despite the fact that the two men shared a love for technology and innovation, in the early days of the computing revolution they couldn't have been further apart in terms of personality. While Jobs was a showman through and through, with a big personality to match, Gates was an engineer at heart, much more introspective and shy. Despite those differences, the two men frequently crossed paths as their companies grew into major players in the personal computing space.

The origin of the rivalry between Gates and Jobs dates back to the early 1980s. At the time, Apple was developing the Macintosh, which would become the first mainstream computer to use a graphical user interface (GUI) for its operating system. Jobs hoped to convince Gates to create software for the new machine, so he gave a demo of the Mac's capabilities to several Microsoft executives, who came away rightfully impressed.

Gates promised to support the Macintosh, while at the same time hatching a plan to create a new operating system of his own. A shrewd evaluator of technology, Gates realized that Apple was charting a course for the future of personal computing and that a graphical interface would appeal to a much larger audience, bringing technology to users who weren't especially tech-savvy.

"

Every strike brings
me closer to the next
home run."

—Babe Ruth

The Macintosh debuted in 1984 to much fanfare but not a lot of success. Its GUI interface may have been revolutionary, but software developers were slow to adapt to the new paradigm. However, true to his word, Gates delivered Microsoft Word and MultiPlan for Apple's new platform, providing the promised support.

While Microsoft continued to develop software for the Mac, it was also pushing forward with Gate's plan for a new graphical operating system that it could bring to the market. In 1985, the company announced the first version of Windows, which was slow and clunky compared to Apple's OS but offered much of the same functionality.

Naturally, Jobs was incensed. He accused Gates of stealing the Mac's "look and feel" and vowed to fight Microsoft in court. He took every opportunity to deride his competitor for being un-original and uninspired despite the fact that Apple had gotten the idea for the GUI from Xerox while developing the Macintosh a few years earlier. None of that mattered to Jobs, however, who saw the move on the part of Gates as a betrayal of the highest level.

In 1988, Apple sued Microsoft on the grounds that it had copied the Mac operating system, but by that time Jobs was no longer with the company; he had been fired a few years earlier due to an intense showdown with CEO John Sculley. Jobs had personally recruited and hired Sculley to run Apple, but the two men often found themselves at loggerheads over key strategic decisions.

After four years of battling it out in court, Microsoft was awarded a major victory. The judge ruled that Apple couldn't patent or protect the idea of a graphical user interface, clearing the way for Gates and his team of engineers to continue developing and selling their operating system. In time, Gates's intuition about the rise of the GUI would prove accurate, and within a few years Windows would become the most dominant OS in the world, far out-pacing the Macintosh.

By the time that happened, Jobs had already founded a new hardware and software company called NeXT. That start-up was also focused on creating a powerful and flexible new operating system that used a graphical interface, copying much of what Jobs and his team had learned while at Apple.

Of course, that didn't mean that he was ready to bury the hatchet with Gates.

In the years that followed, Jobs took every opportunity he could to blast Microsoft and its cofounder. In one interview he proclaimed that if NeXT didn't win the war against its rivals, personal computers would enter a "dark age." In another article, he complained that Microsoft made "third-rate products." He even said the company "had no taste" and that "they don't think of original ideas, and they don't bring much culture into their products."

By the mid-1990s, the rivalry between Jobs and Gates was still going strong, although the one between Apple and Microsoft had cooled off considerably. By then, Windows was on nearly every computer sold, while the Mac was floundering badly. In fact, it had even gotten to the point where Apple was on the verge of bankruptcy and was in serious need of help.

At one point, Apple was struggling with its software effort. The company's then-CEO Gil Amelio reached out to Jobs about acquiring NeXT, but before the deal went through, Gates reportedly told

Amelio that he thought he was making a big mistake and that the NeXT operating system was all flash and no substance. He also blasted Jobs, saying that he didn't know anything about technology. At the time it seemed that the feud was as bitter as ever.

Despite Gates's warning, Apple did buy NeXT and welcomed Jobs back into the fold more than a decade after he was sent into exile. The technology that came along with him became the foundation for the modern Macintosh operating system and played a role in the creation of the software that runs on the iPhone and a plethora of other Apple gadgets. But before that could happen, the company's co-founder had to find a way to save the company he had started, which meant putting an end to his fight with Gates once and for all.

It wasn't long after Apple acquired NeXT that Gil Amelio was out as CEO and Jobs took over the company once again. But he had inherited a sinking ship that looked as though it could go out of business within a matter of weeks. He knew that he had to do something and do it quickly, or Apple would disappear from the tech landscape, most likely for good.

Hat in hand, Jobs, looking for a lifeline, reached out to his rival in the summer of 1997. He asked Gates to invest in Apple, giving the company the chance to come back from the brink. For his part, Gates was magnanimous as the two tech luminaries set aside their long-standing feud to come together at long last.

Knowing that the Mac was an important platform for Microsoft, the company ended up investing $150 million in Apple and its returning CEO. That was enough to buy Jobs some time to help right the ship, eventually returning Apple to profitability and turning it into one of the most innovative tech companies on the planet. Under his watch, the Mac became a popular computer once again, and he introduced a string of successful products that included the iPod, iPhone, and iPad.

Years later, Gates and Jobs would sit down for a joint interview in which they talked about what it was like to finally get past their differences. In that interview, which took place at the D5 tech conference and was conducted by Walt Mossberg of the *Wall Street Journal,* Jobs said, "Apple was in very serious trouble. And what was really clear was that if the game was a zero-sum game where for Apple to win, Microsoft had to lose, then Apple was going to lose." He went on to add, "To me, it was pretty essential to break that paradigm."

The Gates vs. Jobs rivalry is a good reminder of what happens when we continue to fight a battle for far longer than we should. In this case, that fight lasted for years although the end result was the same. Both sides wasted time and energy waging a war that ultimately was counterproductive for both.

66

Holding on to anger
is like drinking poison
and expecting the other
person to die."

—Buddha

It is also a good example of how we should never allow the battles we choose to fight to interfere with the relationships we have with others. Had Jobs known that he would need assistance from Microsoft at some point, he likely would have been much more measured in his criticisms. On the other hand, had Gates been willing to hold on to the grudge, he could have chosen not to invest his company's money in Apple, letting his competitor go out of business instead. Fortunately, that isn't what happened, and one of the biggest rivalries in the history of business came to an end as a result.

Most of us probably won't find ourselves in a clash that impacts the fate of two of the most valuable companies in the world, but the lessons remain the same. Be respectful, stick to your proper rules of engagement, and don't continue the fight longer than you need to. When possible, look for options that are beneficial for everyone involved, and you may find that you can score a win even when things haven't necessarily gone your way.

Fighting the good fight means knowing that you've drawn that proverbial line in the sand and taken a stand on an important topic while still finding a way to come out with your character and reputation intact. We all have to choose the battles that are important to us from time to time, but that doesn't mean we have to take a scorched earth approach to fighting them. At the end of the day, it doesn't necessarily matter what the outcome of that conflict ends up being, provided you can look at yourself in the mirror knowing that you conducted yourself with professionalism and class every step of the way.

PART III

WINNING THE BATTLE

Navy SEALs have a motto, "All in, all the time." This means that no matter what you're doing in your life, you should be prepared to give that activity or project all of the attention, time, and energy that it needs to see it successfully through to the end. This mindset, paired with the SEALs' legendary work ethic, is part of what sets them apart from any other military unit, allowing them to achieve extraordinary things through focus, mental toughness, and an unrelenting will to win the day—every day.

Even after he has successfully completed BUD/S, a SEAL knows that his training is only just beginning. In fact, he is embarking on a lifelong process that involves not just honing his existing skills but constantly learning new ones as well. In this way, he can prepare for whatever challenges that come along, and in the process increase the likelihood that he will prevail when called upon to do his job.

Nowhere is this more evident than in the story of the hijacking of the *Maersk Alabama*, which took place off the coast of Somalia in April of 2009. At the time, the cargo vessel was en route to Kenya after departing from port in Oman. As it sailed down the African coast, the ship was boarded by Somali pirates while in international waters, becoming the first American-flagged vessel to be seized by buccaneers in nearly two hundred years.

The gunmen stormed the *Maersk Alabama* and quickly took over the bridge, but not before the crew disabled the ship's controls in order to prevent the pirates from taking it back to Somalia. Some members of the crew even managed to capture the leader of the boarding party and attempted to use him as a bargaining chip to secure the release of their commander, Captain Richard Phillips. That trade went awry when the pirates refused to comply with their agreement, instead taking Phillips captive and fleeing the cargo vessel in a captured lifeboat.

A day later, the USS *Bainbridge* and *Halyburton* arrived on the scene and escorted the *Maersk Alabama* safely to its destination. The two warships were armed with sophisticated modern weaponry that would make short work of any Somali vessels that ventured too close, so the rest of the voyage went by without incident. With the cargo ship out of danger, the two US naval vessels turned their attention to rescuing Captain Phillips from his Somali captors.

It didn't take long to find the lifeboat containing the pirates and their American hostage. The tiny craft was making its way across the Indian Ocean in an attempt to reach the coast of Somalia. The plan was to turn Phillips over to a group of terrorists who were holding other kidnapped individuals in a secure place on shore. Before that could happen, the *Bainbridge* and *Halyburton* moved in to block their progress.

66

There is no secret to success. It is the result of preparation, hard work, and learning from failure."

—General Colin Powell

Over the next few days, a tense standoff took place, with the Somalis opening fire on the American warships anytime they drew too close. Hostage negotiators attempted to diffuse the situation and get the pirates to release Phillips, but the two sides soon found themselves at a stalemate. The lifeboat had run out of fuel and was unable to finish its journey home, but the US warships weren't about to assist their adversaries so long as they held Phillips captive. Neither side seemed willing to concede an inch.

As the first day of the hostage standoff was unfolding off the coast of Africa, a team of Navy SEALs assigned to Team Six was dispatched from Virginia. The six men were flown halfway around the globe only to parachute into the water with an inflatable boat and make their way to the *Bainbridge* where they were ordered to play a support role as required. The negotiators were still hoping for a peaceful end to the situation, but the SEALs were a good insurance policy just in case things went south.

As the days passed tensions between the two sides continued to mount. At one point, one of the pirates requested medical attention and was brought aboard the *Bainbridge* for treatment, effectively surrendering himself into American custody. Meanwhile, his three friends who were still aboard the lifeboat were as hostile and belligerent as ever, regularly making boisterous and threatening gestures toward the enemy.

The SEALs aboard the *Bainbridge* took up positions on the ship that allowed them to observe the lifeboat at all times. Their rules of engagement didn't allow them to use deadly force to rescue Phillips unless his life was in immediate danger. The SEALs patiently waited and watched, ready to assist at a moment's notice if called upon.

On the fourth day of the standoff, unbeknownst to US forces, Phillips attempted to escape, wrestling with one of his captors in a bid to get away. During the exchange, a weapon was inadvertently fired into the water, bringing a quick end to the skirmish. That same gunshot managed to put the SEALs on high alert as well. Their experience told them that if they didn't act soon things could go very badly for the captured American ship captain.

From then on, the SEALs kept constant surveillance on the lifeboat, waiting for just the right moment to present itself. That moment came after sunset, when all three Somali pirates were visible aboard the small boat at the exact same time. One of the men was threatening Phillips with a rifle, which meant the American's life was indeed in danger. Using night-vision scopes attached to their sniper rifles, the SEALs executed three simultaneous shots to the heads of their adversaries. In the blink of an eye, the pirates were dead, the standoff was over, and Captain Phillips was a free man.

The story of the rescue of Richard Phillips is a great example of how constant training and meticulous preparation helps the Navy SEALs to be the absolute best at what they do. Not only are these men constantly training to be as physically and mentally fit as possible, but they also learn to work together as part of a closely-knit team. This allows a group of individuals who are highly skilled on their own, to be even more effective when they find ways to collaborate. In other words, a SEAL team is more than the sum of its parts simply because each man is committed to constantly learning, adapting, and improving, making himself a more useful teammate in every way. Working individually, or together, they are all in, all the time.

The SEALs who were dispatched to assist in the Captain Phillips hostage standoff left Virginia and flew eight thousand miles nonstop to the Indian Ocean, with their aircraft refueling three times while in flight. They reached their designated drop zone well after midnight, made a high altitude, low opening (HALO) parachute jump, splashing down in turbulent waters under the cover of darkness. They then boarded their inflatable boat and rendezvoused with the *Bainbridge* without the enemy ever knowing they were there.

Later, when called upon, the three SEALs each made absolutely incredible sniper shots at the exact same moment. That alone is a testament to their intense training, but when you consider that they also had to take into account the speed and direction of the wind, not to mention the movement of the ship and lifeboat on the open ocean, you quickly gain a new appreciation for the level of skill involved. The precision required to pull all of that off is difficult to overstate, allowing the SEALs to end the standoff quickly and efficiently, saving the life of the hostage in the process.

Unlike Navy SEALs, most people don't have to face life or death circumstances when it comes to fighting their battles. In fact, it's usually quite the contrary, as most of the conflicts that we face on a regular basis are much more personal in nature. However, that doesn't mean that there isn't a lot at stake with real-world consequences that have a dramatic impact on our lives or those around us. That gives us a real incentive to avoid losing those battles whenever possible.

When a SEAL is sent into combat, he is more than likely the best trained and prepared individual on the battlefield. Usually he is outfitted with some of the most advanced weapons and technology available and has trained above and beyond anything that his adversary has ever considered. Despite all of that, he knows that no outcome is ever assured. There are always unforeseen variables that can cause things to go awry, and while he has contingency plans to deal with the changing conditions of combat, victory is never a foregone conclusion.

It is important that we keep this in mind when choosing our battles as well. No matter how much we do our homework, look for ways to cooperatively engage with our opponents, and seek creative solutions to problems, there is still no way to guarantee that we'll come out ahead in the end. That said, there are certainly some tactics that we can use to help give us an edge.

Much like Navy SEALs, the more you sweat in your training, the less blood you'll shed in combat. In this case, that means being as prepared as you can be in order to avoid the possibility that you might end up losing your battle. For instance, it helps to thoroughly understand both sides of a debate or to have a firm grasp of what your opponent's objectives are too. It means having an empathetic understanding of where those on the other side of a conflict stand, while offering well-thought-out ideas and solutions that can help to resolve differences. By coming to the boardroom, office, or kitchen table as prepared as possible, you'll have a better chance of achieving whatever it is you've set out to accomplish.

"

Do not follow where
the path may lead.
Go instead where
there is no path and
leave a trail."

— Ralph Waldo Emerson

As important as planning and preparation can be, there is more to winning your battles than just doing your homework. For instance, it helps if you can take a leadership role when it comes to looking for constructive ways to resolve differences and find solutions. Too often we are quick to criticize the opposition, or we get overly defensive, lashing out at those who may not agree with our point of view. But those aren't constructive methods for finding common ground. Instead, we should avoid those kinds of traps and look for ways to productively navigate through the minefield that separates us from those on the other side.

It is not uncommon for us to find ourselves bogged down in a battle just because no one is willing to step up and assume a leadership role. Sometimes this happens because we want to avoid seeming overly aggressive or because we don't want to be perceived as stepping on anyone's toes. At other times, it is because we're not really sure how to proceed or we're expecting someone else to take control instead.

More often than not, we lack leadership in a conflict for one simple reason—we actually lack a leader. Taking charge means having to assume the burden of responsibility, which most people look to avoid. But if you want to find a resolution to your battle, especially one that is favorable to your cause, you increase your chances of success simply by taking the reins and guiding the direction of the discussion.

There is a line in the Navy SEAL creed that reads: "We expect to lead and be led. In the absence of orders I will take charge, lead my teammates and accomplish the mission. I lead by example in all situations." This is an approach that we can easily adopt when it comes to resolving the conflicts and battles that we face in our lives too.

There will be times when someone is willing to lead the way and we should be supportive of those efforts. However, when there is a void in leadership, we shouldn't hesitate to assume that role ourselves. If the battles that we choose to fight really are important to us on a personal level, why would we want to rely on anyone else to see them through to their conclusion? By stepping into the leadership position we can assert more control over the direction that the conversation goes, potentially steering it in one that is more favorable to our point of view.

That said, it is important to adhere to the final line of that quote from the SEAL creed as well. The part that says we should lead by example. That means that even though we are assuming the role of the leader, we should also hold ourselves to a high standard of conduct at all times. We can do that by allowing the opposition plenty of time to be heard, making them feel like they are part of the conversation and giving them a chance to assist in shaping any potential solutions. While it's true that we can certainly influence the results of a conflict by taking charge of the situation, if we want to resolve the showdown in a productive manner, it is important that we are fair and balanced in our approach.

Defining and adhering to our rules of engagement are even more important when we are leading by example. Remaining respectful and accommodating to all parties involved will help lessen the levels of tension and keep the lines of communication flowing. Some will likely be suspicious of our motives, but by assuring them that we remain focused on finding a solution to the challenges at hand we can hopefully build a level of trust that allows us to get through the process without negatively impacting our relationships.

When playing the role of a leader, it is important to remain focused on potential solutions as much as possible. Some of the individuals who are engaged in the conflict may find themselves getting emotional at times, particularly if the topic is one that holds significant value to them. They may lash out in anger or feel frustrated by the direction or pace that things take. Those are natural human emotions that tend to flare up when defending something that we care deeply about. It is good to acknowledge those feelings and try to understand where they are coming from, but they can also be counterproductive when it comes to finding a resolution that is equitable to everyone involved.

Allowing others to provide their input is vital to reaching a consensus and finding a viable outcome. Emotional outbursts and fiery arguments don't contribute to that process, however, so while they are likely to happen from time to time, we can't let ourselves be pulled into that trap. Avoid those types of quagmires by steering the conversation back toward a more goal-oriented discussion that encourages all involved to offer potential solutions. In this way, we're always working toward an endpoint rather than continuously getting caught up in petty squabbles that distract us from the goal.

When it comes to finding solutions to any conflict, proposing outcomes that are favorable for everyone involved is usually the surest way to find success. This seems like a logical approach of course, but when it comes to divvying up resources or finding common ground, we can end up being incredibly territorial. There will be times when it will be difficult to convince the parties involved that it is better to score a smaller win for everyone than it is to achieve an overwhelming victory for one side that leaves the other with nothing. This is especially true if any of the participants in the conflict are feeling marginalized, unheard, or squeezed out. When that happens they may decide to dig their heels in even deeper, making your job an even more difficult one.

It takes more to win your battles than simply assuming the leadership role. Although it is indeed a step in the right direction, you may find that someone else wants to step up to fill that position or your foe may be unwilling to concede the leadership mantle to someone from the opposing side. When this occurs you may find yourself locked in a struggle for control, which ultimately can be a major distraction that takes time and effort away from solving the actual conflict that you're trying to resolve.

"

You may have to fight
a battle more than once
to win it."

—Margaret Thatcher

t is important that you don't allow yourself to get too caught up in those kinds of disputes. It is still possible to achieve your goals and display leadership even if someone else is directing the tone and tempo of the conversation. Just don't lose sight of the things that you want to accomplish and be sure that your opinions and insights are being heard. With a well-thought-out strategy, a respectful approach when dealing with others, and a plan for achieving a solution, you can still have a dramatic influence on which direction the conflict goes.

Whether you're directly leading the discussion or just playing a role in finding a viable solution, patience will likely be vital to finding success. There will be times when you'll need to remind yourself that not every conflict can be resolved as quickly as we'd like, particularly if your opponents are feeling as passionate about the issues as you are. Sorting through potential options and discussing outcomes that can be beneficial for everyone can take time. Keep this in mind if you start to feel frustrated with the lack of progress.

Remaining patient will also help us avoid rushing into a solution that may not be beneficial to your needs. While it is always important to be continually working toward a conclusion to the battle, we should remind ourselves from time to time that it isn't just about putting an end to the conflict, even though there may be times when that is precisely what we want to do the most.

Remember, if we chose to draw a line in the sand over a particular issue, it was probably for a very good reason. Don't let all of your time and effort go to waste just because you're in a hurry to put the fight behind you. Hasty decisions can have unintended consequences later, including the lasting regret that comes from not standing your ground when you had the chance.

Seeing any battle through to the end is an important part of being successful, plus we may not ever get the opportunity to take a stand on an important topic again. You've picked your battles wisely for a reason, so don't give up simply because it is taking longer than you expected to find a conclusion.

If you're not prepared to stay in the fight until it has come to its logical end you may eventually look back on it as a missed opportunity. One in which you burned a lot of time and energy, only to bail out before the battle was over. Win or lose, it is important to be patient and allow things to progress at their natural pace. Not doing so could potentially end up costing you valuable credibility along the way. It can be difficult for others to take us seriously when we choose to pick a fight on an important topic, only to give up when things aren't progressing as quickly as we'd like.

Creating a list of priorities and developing a course of action can help us maintain our patience when things start to drag on. By creating a plan designed to lead us to a solution, we can turn our attention away from the bigger picture for a time and concentrate on the micro-goals that we need to accomplish to make progress toward our much bigger macro-goal. This can give us the sense that we are still on track even if it seems like things may have slowed down to a crawl.

A good plan of action can play an essential role in winning any battle, which is why it is important to prioritize the things that are most important to you early on. That said, another SEAL mantra says, "No plan survives first contact with the enemy." In other words, no matter how much you prepare, consider your strategy, and focus on your course of action, there's a good chance your opposition will still throw you a curveball. Expect the unexpected and be willing to be flexible with your plans. Chances are, they may not survive first contact with the enemy either.

SEALs overcome these unexpected obstacles by having a set of contingency plans in place that they can fall back on when things inevitably deviate from the original course of action. This gives them the ability to remain nimble and decisive, quickly pivoting to a new tactic as the battle plays out. In doing so, SEALs increase their chances of success simply by assuming that their original plan may not allow them to fully achieve their objectives in the first place. To overcome any mishaps or misfortunes that may come along the way, they are already considering alternative routes to reaching their goals even before new obstacles have presented themselves.

We can all adopt a similar approach when fighting our personal battles. Expecting any conflict to go exactly according to plan is a sure way to set ourselves up for failure. There is a very good chance that our opponents are developing their own plans for how to win the battle too and they more than likely will run counter to whatever it is we have in mind. By understanding how our opponents are thinking, we can begin to get an idea of what their plans might be, allowing us to anticipate how they'll approach the conflict. This allows us to start forming contingencies and giving us the ability to anticipate the most likely points of contention and potentially formulate ways to negotiate around them. The goal, of course, is to find a solution that is equitable for everyone involved.

There have been countless negotiations throughout history that have pitted two sides against one another as they strived to resolve some important conflict. Few of those have had such high stakes—and potentially dire consequences—as the Cuban Missile Crisis. For thirteen days in 1962 the world watched as the US and the Soviet Union played a game of chess with one another, with the threat of nuclear holocaust hanging overhead. However, in the end, both sides were able to negotiate a compromise that was beneficial to each, while avoiding a conflict that could have resulted in the death of tens of millions of people.

Following the end of World War II, the US and the Soviets found themselves as the two remaining superpowers. In the years that followed, the former allies squared off with one another in a cold war that only caused animosity and tensions between the two nations to grow. Both sides entered into an arms race that included building a massive stockpile of nuclear weapons and fighting proxy wars against one another around the globe. And while American soldiers never directly met Russian forces on the battlefield, it seemed like only a matter of time before such a showdown would occur.

"

Every accomplishment
starts with the
decision to try."

— John F. Kennedy

As that arms race continued, the US placed nuclear missiles in Italy and Turkey, which was close enough to the USSR to strike important targets with only a few minutes' warning. Naturally, this didn't sit well with Soviet Premier Nikita Khrushchev, who saw the weapons as a serious threat to the security of his nation. In order to counter that threat, he entered into negations with Cuban leader Fidel Castro, who had led a communist takeover of that country just a few years earlier.

During his rise to power, Castro had overthrown a government that had been friendly to the US and created a communist regime just ninety miles off the coast of Florida. He had also survived several attempts to remove him from power, including a failed invasion by Cuban nationals at the Bay of Pigs in 1961. By accepting Khrushchev's offer of placing nuclear weapons inside his country, Castro was also creating a deterrent against any future aggression from the US.

In October of 1962, a U-2 spy plane took photos of Russian forces assembling medium and intermediate-range missiles on Cuban soil. This immediately led to a naval blockade of the island that was designed to prevent further weapons from being deployed within the Caribbean nation. This led to a tense standoff as a Russian fleet carrying more nuclear missiles and Soviet personnel sped toward Cuba, while US naval ships held their ground, preparing to engage with them on the open ocean.

Both sides of the conflict ratcheted up their rhetoric over the following days. President John F. Kennedy condemned the presence of the missiles in Cuba and called for their immediate removal, while Khrushchev declared the naval blockade an act of war. Neither side was willing to back down as American and Soviet forces seemed destined to directly engage one another for the very first time.

While these events played out on the world stage, allies of both the US and the Soviet Union watched the proceedings closely. The concern was that a naval battle in the Caribbean could escalate to all-out war, which meant the potential use of nuclear weapons. Even in the early 1960s experts knew that such an exchange could lead to the destruction of the planet, which meant that millions of lives were hanging in the balance.

Despite the public posturing from the leaders of both nations, behind the scenes Kennedy and Khrushchev were desperately searching for a peaceful solution that would allow both sides to save face. The two men knew that a military showdown wasn't in the best interest of anyone, but they had to extricate themselves from the clash without losing face at the same time. That meant finding a solution that would work well for everyone involved.

Using backchannel methods of communication, the two sides began exploring ways that they could avoid the Cold War suddenly becoming incredibly hot. The idea was floated that the Soviets would dismantle and remove the missiles from Cuba—under supervision of the United Nations—in exchange for an assurance from Kennedy that the US would not invade the island in an attempt to overthrow Castro. It was also agreed that American missiles in Turkey would be removed at a later date as a way to reduce the growing tensions between the superpowers.

Eventually, Khrushchev and Kennedy struck an agreement and the Russian ships turned around, averting a showdown with their American counterparts. In the weeks that followed, the missiles were dismantled and removed from Cuban soil, while months later the US quietly pulled its missiles from Turkey as well. These actions helped diffuse what had been a growing powder keg and brought an end to the most dangerous game of chicken that the world has ever known.

The conflicts that we choose to take a stand on aren't likely to be as high-stakes as the Cuban Missile Crisis, but there are still plenty of things that we can learn from examining the historic showdown. Upon discovering nuclear weapons in Cuba—just ninety miles from American soil—President Kennedy drew a hard, uncompromising line in the sand. He made it known that the US would not allow missiles to be built so close to its borders and that he would take drastic measures to remove those weapons.

Khrushchev couldn't risk looking weak and losing face within his own government, so he took a stand as well. By ordering the Soviet ships to press on toward the Caribbean, even though that meant a potential armed conflict with the American navy, he, too, was drawing a line in the sand. He wasn't about to have terms dictated to him by the American president, no matter what the stakes. The result was a standoff that many historians believe put us closer to a nuclear war than any other point in history, with the entire world teetering on the brink.

When the US president and Soviet Premier began negotiating with one another through various agents, each had a plan of action in mind for what they wanted to accomplish. For Kennedy it was the immediate removal of the missiles from Cuba, while Khrushchev looked to protect his new Cuban ally. He also hoped to get the US to dismantle some of its nuclear arsenals as well, which would be viewed as a significant win back home in the Kremlin. Neither side wanted to appear weak nor look like they were conceding to the other, so the process was a delicate one to negotiate.

In the end, the agreement that was reached proved to be beneficial for all involved. American and Russian negotiators managed to turn a negative-sum game (potential nuclear war) into a positive-sum outcome. In exchange for removing the missiles and Russian personnel from Cuba, Khrushchev received assurances from the US that it would not invade Caribbean country.

Meanwhile, Kennedy achieved his goal of eliminating a nuclear threat so close to US borders, while also appearing to stand up to the Russians. His concession on dismantling the missiles in Turkey wasn't revealed until much later, which made it seem that the president hadn't given in to his Soviet counterpart at all. At the height of the Cold War that was a major victory for the Kennedy administration, which was already looking ahead to the next election.

66

Victory belongs to the
most persevering."

—Napoleon Bonaparte

At the end of the day, a world crisis was averted and both sides managed to gain increased safety and security for their citizens. In the process, they also learned something about one another too, which helped improve communications during future engagements. In fact, following the Cuban Missile Crisis the US and Soviet Union jointly developed the Moscow-Washington hotline, which allowed the president and the premier to speak directly to one another without the need for intermediaries. The so-called "red phone" has been used to avoid escalating conflicts across the globe ever since.

The negotiations that took place to end the Cuban Missile Crisis are a textbook example of how to successfully reach an endpoint for a very contentious conflict. Both sides managed to achieve their goals, while avoiding losing face at the same time. A conscious effort was made to resolve the issue in a timely manner with neither party feeling like it had been forced to concede on any important points. It was truly a back and forth discussion that led to a victory of sorts for both sides, while avoiding potentially disastrous consequences. Kennedy and Khrushchev were able to navigate that tricky minefield and find a solution that worked for everyone involved, averting the threat of nuclear war in the process.

Knowing when to choose your battles, how to fight them in a respectful and honorable fashion, and having the focus and discipline to push through to the finish line all play an important role in securing victory in any conflict. That said, there will likely be times when it will feel as though the deck is stacked against you and you're fighting that battle both uphill and against the wind. Tenacity and discipline can help us overcome those challenges, allowing us to push forward even when it seems as though things aren't necessarily going our way.

The SEAL creed has a section that addresses this very thing: "I will never quit. I persevere and thrive on adversity. My Nation expects me to be physically harder and mentally stronger than my enemies. If knocked down, I will get back up, every time. I will draw on every remaining ounce of strength to protect my teammates and to accomplish our mission. I am never out of the fight."

Recognizing that we are never truly out of the fight may be the ultimate key to success when it comes to fighting our battles. Just be sure to keep in mind that it is always extremely difficult to beat anyone who refuses to give up, even in the face of mounting adversity. Don't quit. Persevere and you will find a way to thrive.

In the end, there is never a surefire path to victory when it comes to fighting our battles. However, we can increase our chances of coming out on top of the fights that matter the most by choosing those battles wisely, showing our opponents respect and understanding, and taking a leadership role whenever possible.

We'll come out a winner every time if we seek solutions and opportunities rather than look for ways to stand in the path of our adversaries. In doing so, we'll also begin to understand that winning our battles isn't always about getting what we want, but finding a way to ensure a positive outcome not only for ourselves, but for those around us.